Music Minus One Trumpet
or Flugelhorn

BLOWIN' THE BLUES AWAY

mmo

6852

It definitely would be helpful to woodshed the blues scale and phrases from both Mal's line and fragments from my solo to get them "under your fingers"! For example, the alternate fingering phrase with open E and third valve E which allows us trumpeters to pursue the first of the three devices that I'll explore in greater depth at a later time, namely honkin', riffin' and lickin'.

Stay tuned for more on H, R and L.

Hip Tip is an interesting blend of a ballad with bluesy overtones. Although it goes to many places that are not necessarily associated with the blues, it's just that kind of diversion that makes Hip Tip a rewarding musical experience. The Cbs to Bbs anchor it in the blues so I recommend you hover over and re-state those two notes when you solo as I have done to keep it "in the blues bag" where it was intended to be.

With ***Gospel Truth*** we arrive at the very foundation of the blues and jazz itself!

Yes, that was quite a mouthful!

But don't take it lightly for if this element is missing in jazz, in my opinion it tends to be almost, I dare say, un-jazz-like or to put it kindly, jazz without a connection to its roots!

There have always been great improvisors before Jazz appeared and certainly Bach, Mozart and Beethoven had to be among them but I'm certain it could not be classified as Jazz! That's why this Blowin' The Blues Away is such an important milestone as an educational tool. To make this connection with the "roots" of the Blues is vital!

Here's something that needs to be recognized regarding jazz notation: Although we usually accept the approximation of notation in jazz charts and transcriptions of solos, you should realize they are not exact representations as in classical notation. For starters, as is quite evident in the Gospel Truth (an aptly named piece) the rhythm is triplet based. I chose to re-write this in 12/8 time in order to demonstrate the authentic and almost exact representation of this triplet feel that exists most of the time in Classic Jazz. Granted its dominance has been diluted with the entrance of Herbie Hancock's Watermelon Man and Cantaloupe Island and other jazz/rock fusion compositions.

Nuff said! Dig in and get down with the Gospel Truth whether you're a church-goer or not!

Earthy is another minor blues that sits in an easy groove that can "open doors" to a fourth device. Remember the three basic ones are Honkin', Riffin' and Lickin'. (I repeat that because it needs to be installed in your "hard drive") These are essential components of your jazz arsenal a.k.a "bag of tricks".

Enter number four, Suspensions. You'll hear this demonstrated in the opening phrase of my solo with the G and Bb being the obvious suspensions because they are sustained but even scalar passages can create this let's call it irresolution instead of dissonance although you certainly can pursue the Big D (Dissonance).

One of my idols Miles Davis used this device ubiquitously. (Oh, I do love that word!)

Note that my ad lib ending punctuated this with a held, high Bb and yes it's okay not to resolve a suspension!

Our last piece ***Blue Gene*** brings us back to church with again the rhythmical emphasis on triplets. I'd have re-written this one also in 12/8 if it wouldn't have made the notation more complex when transcribing my solo so I stuck with good old 4/4. This requires that you listen and recognize the obvious triplet feel throughout. After all is said and done my ad lib cadenza is the capper for it lands on the bluesy F instead of the tonic G. I call it kind of a Suspension to Nowhere.

Perhaps it could very well anticipate a transition to a volume two of Blowin' The Blues Away where I incorporate some contemporary, smooth jazz and fusion blues.

If you want to communicate with me about anything related to this album feel free to email me at bobzottola@naplesjazzlovers.com.

You're also entitled to a complimentary Skype or FaceTime lesson on this or any other aspect of trumpet playing and improvisation.

Bob Zottola
Naples, Florida

BLOWIN' THE BLUES AWAY

CONTENTS

4

Solo Bb Trumpet or Flugelhorn

The Twister

Mal Waldron

MMO 6852

The Twister

Solo Bb Trumpet or Flugelhorn

Dealin'

Mal Waldron

Dealin'

Solo Bb Trumpet or Flugelhorn

Empty Street

Mal Waldron

Empty Street

Solo Bb Trumpet or Flugelhorn

Blue Greens 'n Beans

Mal Waldron

Blue Greens 'n Beans

Solo Bb Trumpet or Flugelhorn

Hip Tip

Mal Waldron

Hip Tip

Solo Bb Trumpet or Flugelhorn

Gospel Truth

Mal Waldron

Gospel Truth

gradually slowing down _ _ _ _ _ _ _ _ _ _ _ _

Solo Bb Trumpet or Flugelhorn

Earthy

Mal Waldron

Earthy

Solo Bb Trumpet or Flugelhorn

Blue Gene

Mal Waldron

Blue Gene

I was quite happy when asked by Music Minus One to prepare an original album of blues selections, to be performed by a trio and used by various horns as a practicing background. I feel, as do many other musicians, that *blues* are the backbone and source of jazz. Without them and their influence, modern jazz would not have the earthy, funky, swinging feeling that it does and should have. Whenever jazz musicians get together to jam, you will always hear the suggestion, "Let's play some down to earth blues!" Most jazz albums contain one or two blues and unless you can play them you never really make it with the cats.

The *blues* are made up of three basic chords spread out over twelve bars usually. Four bars of the tonic chord (I), two bars of the sub-dominant (IV), two bars of the tonic (I) again, then two bars of the dominant (V), and finally two more bars of the tonic (I). There are many variations of this pattern and I have included some in this album. One popular variation is the breakup of the first four bars as follows: one bar of tonic (I), one bar of sub- dominant (IV), one bar of tonic (I) followed by one bar of tonic (I) with the minor seventh added.

Other variations consist of making the tonic and sub dominant chords minor. This gives us the minor blues illustrated by *Earthy* in this album. Included in this variation is the practice of breaking up the last two bars of the twelve bar blues as follows: one bar tonic (I) minor, and ending with one bar sub-dominant (IV) minor.

The blues also get their quality from the melodic pattern which is based on the minor scales. These scales contain lowered thirds, sevenths, and sixths. The use of these scales plus the inclusion of "blue" notes gives us our blues quality. "Blue" notes refer to notes played out of pitch or flat. Some "blue" notes are flattened as far as a half step lower. The use of the flatted fifth in blues is an example of that.

I have put the blues contained in this album into four categories,

1.) Ballad Blues	*2.) Church Type Blues*	*3.) Minor Blues*	*4.) Back-beat Groove Blues*

1. BALLAD BLUES: a. *Hip Tip* is slow and gets its ballad feeling through its tempo and construction. It consists of eight bars (A) another similar eight bars (A) then a bridge, an eight bar sections of new material (B) and finally another eight bars similar to the beginning(A). The blues feeling comes from the tonic dominant stress in the outside eights and the sub-dominant stress in the bridge. Added blues feeling comes from the melodic use of the tonic, sub-dominant and dominant.

2. CHURCH TYPE BLUES: a. *Gospel Truth* is an example of the type of blues heard in Negro Churches. It is really a jazz blues but I've given it the older feeling heard in these churches. It is slow and has a basic eight bar construction which is followed by a similar eight bars that contains melodic variations and the climax of the tune. The three basic blues chords, tonic, sub-dominant and dominant are placed in key positions to bring out the blues quality. Notice in the ninth bar the use of the tonic chord for two beats and the dominant chord for two beats. This device really gives us the old-time blues feeling. The triplet feeling on each beat in the rhythm gives *Gospel Truth* its final strong church quality.

b. *Blue Gene* is very similar in feeling to the tune above. The construction here is the basic blues form outlined in my second paragraph. The melody outlines the basic changes and the church quality comes out in the melody and rhythmic background.

3. MINOR BLUES: a. *Earthy* is a minor blues of the construction pointed our in my third paragraph. Many musicians feel that the minor blues were the first blues ever used. They certainly give a strong, forceful and direct feeling to the listener. *Earthy* contains a decided emphasis on the flatted fifth and ends rather mournfully on the sub-dominant (IV).

b. *Dealin'* is an example of a modern minor blues. It has a basic blues form of twelve bars and uses the three basic blues changes but the melody makes the big difference. The melody hovers around the minor seventh and flatted ninth of the chord and by so doing, gives the music a two key feeling! The chords move in F and the melody moves in Eb minor. The tune also ends rather differently on the sub-dominant (IV).

4. BACK-BEAT GROOVE BLUES: a. *Twister* is actually a rhythm and blues tune. It has the "I Got Rhythm" changes of a rhythm tune and the melodic stress on minor thirds, minor sevenths, and "Blue" notes, of a blues. The back-beat (strong accent on beats two and four) completes the picture.

b. *Blue Greens N' Beans* is a basic twelve bar blues with basic blues chord progressions and a back-beat. It ends on a sub-dominant chord (IV) for variety.

Mal Waldron was born in New York City on August 16th, 1926. At ten he began to study the piano, classics only. His father had studied the violin as a boy but an accident to his hand forced him to stop. He subsequently and avidly collected records of classical music, a practice he still pursues.

Mal's interest in jazz started around 1939. In 1941 he started playing alto saxophone with neighborhood groups. In 1944 he was drafted, and played sax with stateside jazz units within his outfit. It was at this time that Mal started writing tunes and small arrangements. He also switched back to the piano at this time. In 1947, on release from the service, he entered Queens College, choosing music as his major. He studied composition with Dr. Karol Rathaus in 1948 and graduated in June 1949 with a B.A. in music education. It was at this time that Mal started writing scores for Modern Dancers and Modern Ballet Dancers. He wrote music primarily for the Henry Street Playhouse under Alwin Nikolais, while also doing scores for Florita Raup and Fred Berk (Choreographers). During 1950- 1951 he again studied composition with Dr. Rathaus. It was at this time that jazz gigs started coming his way, and during the period 1950-1954 he worked with Kansas Fields, Ike Quebec and Big Nick Nicholas. From 1954- 1957 he worked with Charlie Mingus' groups, while also working with Lucky Thompson, Howard McGhee, Allan Eager, Gigi Gryce, Teddy Charles, Jackie McLean and Gene Ammons.

Mal has recorded for Prestige, Atlantic, Columbia, Verve, Electra, Savoy and Bethlehem. In April of 1957 he became Billie Holiday's accompanist working with Billie until her death in the summer of 1959. He has since then worked with his own trio and quintet.

"You now have all the information that you'll need to work with this album. I hope you enjoy it as much as we enjoyed making it."
- Mal Waldron

Music Minus One
50 Executive Boulevard • Elmsford, New York 10523-1325
914-592-1188 • e-mail: info@musicminusone.com
www.musicminusone.com

MMO 6852

ISBN 978-1-941566-83-1